D1372166

LOOK AT YOUR BODY

BRAIN
AND NERVES

STEVE PARKER

ILLUSTRATED BY IAN THOMPSON

Copper Beech Books
Brookfield, Connecticut

*First published in the
United States in 1998 by*
Copper Beech Books,
an imprint of
The Millbrook Press
2 Old New Milford Road
Brookfield, Connecticut
06804

Printed in Belgium

Editor
Jon Richards
Design
David West
Children's Book Design
Designer Robert Perry
Illustrator
Ian Thompson
Picture Research
Brooks Krikler Research
Consultant
Dr. Rachel Levene
MB.BS, DCH, DRCOG

Library of Congress
Cataloging-in-Publication Data
Parker, Steve.
Brain and nerves / by Steve Parker;
illustrated by Ian Thompson.
p. cm — (Look at your body)
Includes index.
Summary: Looks at how the human
brain works, including memory and
learning as well as brain and
nerve diseases.
ISBN 0-7613-0812-1 (lib. bdg.)
1. Neurophysiology—Juvenile
literature. 2. Nervous system—
Juvenile literature.
[1. Brain. 2. Nervous system.]
I. Thompson, Ian, 1964- ill.
II. Title. III. Series.
QP361.5.P349 1998   97-31925
612.8—dc21   CIP AC
5 4 3 2 1

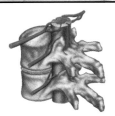

CONTENTS

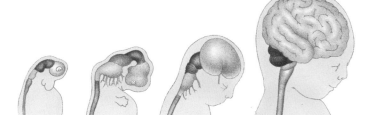

INTRODUCTION

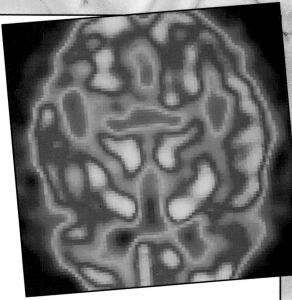

Look at your body! Tap your head. Just under your hair, skin, and bones is your brain. Has it been used today? You do not have to solve a difficult problem or recall a distant memory for your brain to be active. It is busy all the time, even when you are daydreaming, resting, or asleep. It's the control center for the coordination of your whole body. It is in charge of making all body parts and processes work together in a smooth and organized way. It is the site of the thinking mind, with its store of memories and experiences, its ideas and emotions, likes and dislikes, and hopes and dreams.

Running from your brain to all parts of your body are millions and millions of microscopically tiny nerve fibers. These miniature cables carry messages that inform your brain about what is going on and tell your body what to do.

PREHISTORIC BRAINS

Some dinosaurs, such as Diplodocus (below) and Stegosaurus, had tiny brains for their gigantic bodies. Yet they survived for millions of years — far longer than humans have been on the earth. So their brains must have been adequate for the tasks of the time, such as finding food and avoiding predators.

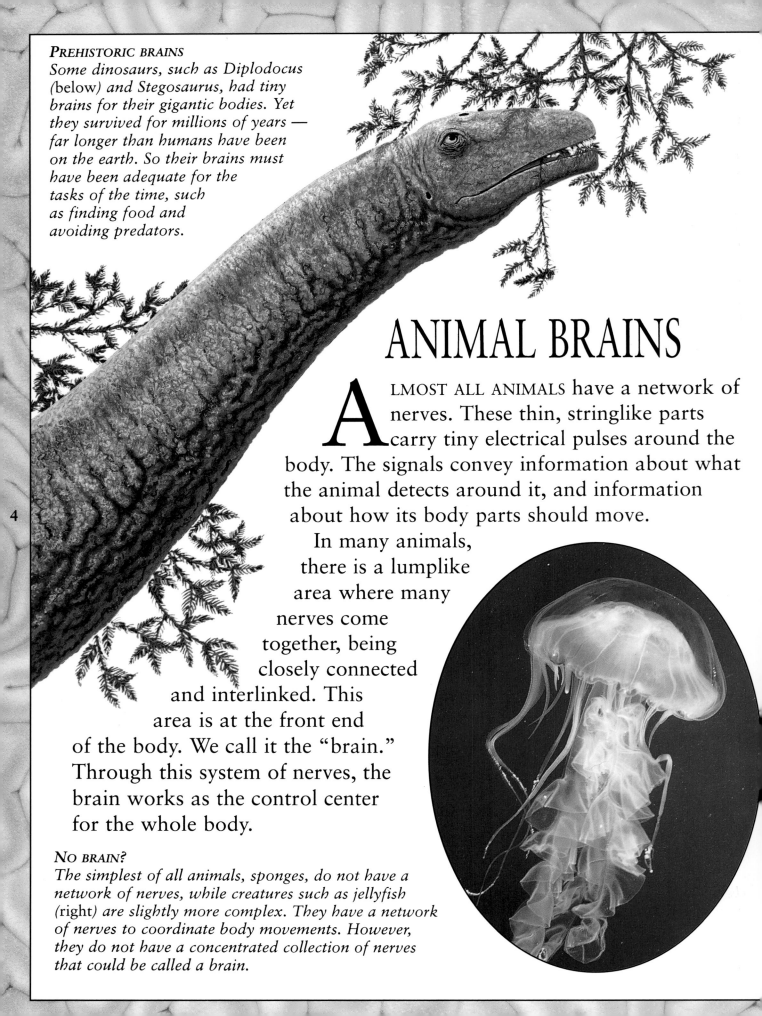

4

ANIMAL BRAINS

ALMOST ALL ANIMALS have a network of nerves. These thin, stringlike parts carry tiny electrical pulses around the body. The signals convey information about what the animal detects around it, and information about how its body parts should move.

In many animals, there is a lumplike area where many nerves come together, being closely connected and interlinked. This area is at the front end of the body. We call it the "brain." Through this system of nerves, the brain works as the control center for the whole body.

NO BRAIN?

The simplest of all animals, sponges, do not have a network of nerves, while creatures such as jellyfish (right) are slightly more complex. They have a network of nerves to coordinate body movements. However, they do not have a concentrated collection of nerves that could be called a brain.

CLEVER CREATURES

Cuttlefish, squid, and octopus (right) are members of the mollusk group (which also includes snails and slugs). They have a large and complex brain for their body size, and show a certain amount of "intelligent behavior." They can learn to recognize patterns, colors, and even numbers of objects.

SEEING WELL

The brains of many creatures have specialized areas to deal with different functions. The olfactory, or smell, area receives signals from the nose about smell (see page 21 to find the olfactory area). The motor area controls the body's muscles, telling the body how to move. The bigger an area of the brain, the greater its importance in the animal's lifestyle. The brain of a chameleon (below) has large optic, or vision, areas, giving it good sight.

THE BIGGEST BRAIN

Bigger brains do not necessarily mean greater intelligence. Also important is the size of the brain compared to the whole body, called the brain:body ratio. The biggest brain in the animal kingdom, weighing around 18 lbs (8 kg), belongs to the sperm whale (right). But its brain:body ratio is only 1:5000, compared to 1:50 for a human.

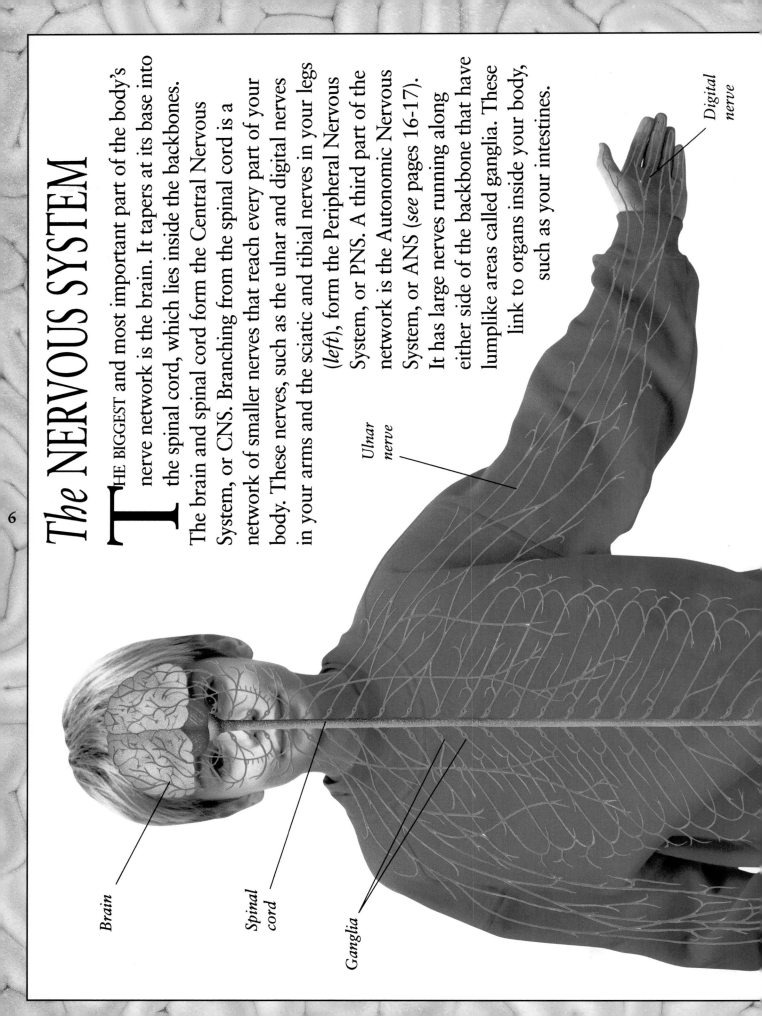

The NERVOUS SYSTEM

THE BIGGEST and most important part of the body's nerve network is the brain. It tapers at its base into the spinal cord, which lies inside the backbones. The brain and spinal cord form the Central Nervous System, or CNS. Branching from the spinal cord is a network of smaller nerves that reach every part of your body. These nerves, such as the ulnar and digital nerves in your arms and the sciatic and tibial nerves in your legs (*left*), form the Peripheral Nervous System, or PNS. A third part of the network is the Autonomic Nervous System, or ANS (*see* pages 16-17). It has large nerves running along either side of the backbone that have lumplike areas called ganglia. These link to organs inside your body, such as your intestines.

Digital
nerve

Ulnar
nerve

Brain

Spinal
cord

Ganglia

6

TO THE BRAIN

Throughout the day, sense organs in your body receive information from the world around you, such as the scent of a flower (below) or the color of a ball. These sense organs then convert this information into tiny electrical signals that pass along the thin nerves to your brain, where the data is decoded and interpreted.

FROM THE BRAIN

As well as receiving information, your brain sends out instructions to the parts of your body, telling it how to behave. These commands travel as tiny electrical signals along the motor nerves to the body's muscles. They tell you how to walk or run, or when to swing the bat in order to hit the ball (below).

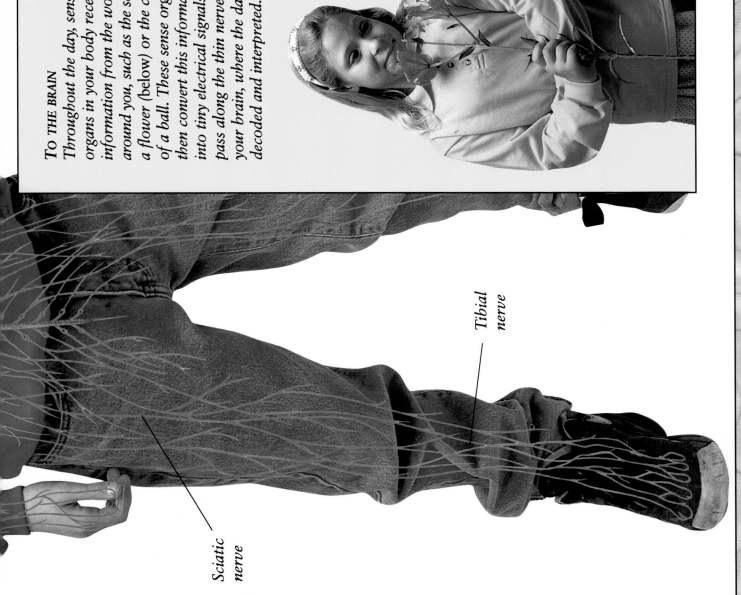

Sciatic nerve

Tibial nerve

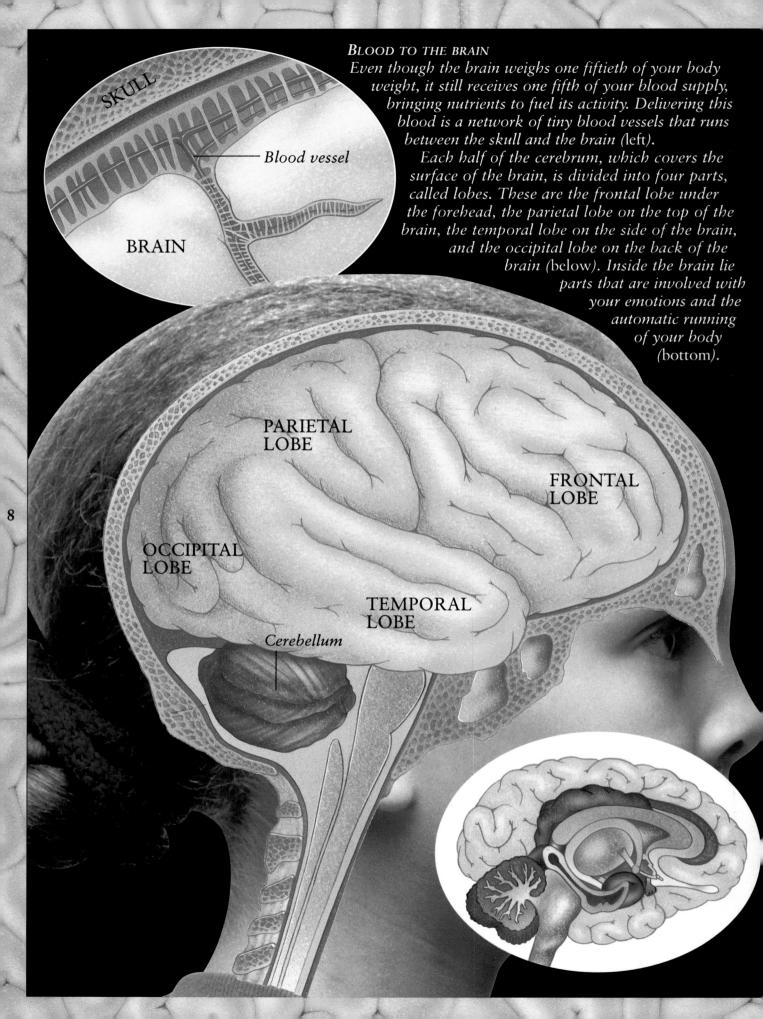

SKULL

Blood vessel

BRAIN

BLOOD TO THE BRAIN
Even though the brain weighs one fiftieth of your body weight, it still receives one fifth of your blood supply, bringing nutrients to fuel its activity. Delivering this blood is a network of tiny blood vessels that runs between the skull and the brain (left).

Each half of the cerebrum, which covers the surface of the brain, is divided into four parts, called lobes. These are the frontal lobe under the forehead, the parietal lobe on the top of the brain, the temporal lobe on the side of the brain, and the occipital lobe on the back of the brain (below). Inside the brain lie parts that are involved with your emotions and the automatic running of your body (bottom).

PARIETAL LOBE

FRONTAL LOBE

OCCIPITAL LOBE

TEMPORAL LOBE

Cerebellum

8

The BRAIN

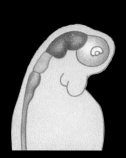

THE HUMAN BRAIN fills the top half of the head. It is soft in texture and weighs about 3 lbs (1.4 kg). From the outside, the brain is divided into two halves, called hemispheres. Each hemisphere is covered by a layer of the brain called the cerebrum. The surface of the cerebrum is heavily wrinkled. This allows more brain cells to be packed into the restricted space inside your head. To the rear of the brain, and tucked in just under the cerebrum, is another part of the brain called the cerebullum (*far left*). Projecting out from just in front of the cerebullum is the long, thin spinal cord that runs down your spine (*see* pages 10-11).

"Seeing" the brain
The brain, being soft tissue, does not show up on an X-ray image. But other methods can help doctors "see" your brain. These include PET scans that monitor the activity of your brain with the help of a radioactive dye (above).

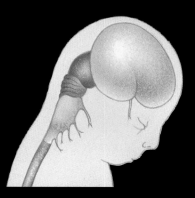

The growing brain
About three weeks after conception (below), a tube of nerve tissue has formed along the back of the embryo. The front of this enlarges and develops three bulges, the forebrain, midbrain, and hindbrain. The rear part of the nerve tube is the spinal cord. The brain's main shape is recognizable after about three months and by birth it has developed its wrinkled surface.

If a small part of one of the arteries supplying blood to the brain expands it can cut off the blood supply to the brain. It can also cause blood to leak out into the layer surrounding the brain (*left*). This is called an aneurysm. The leaked blood can put great pressure on the brain and if this pressure is not released in time it can cause a stroke. Damage can also be caused by a blocked blood vessel, called a thrombosis.

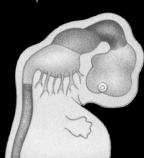

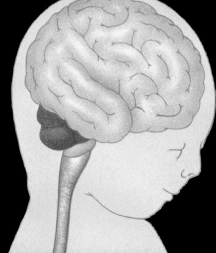

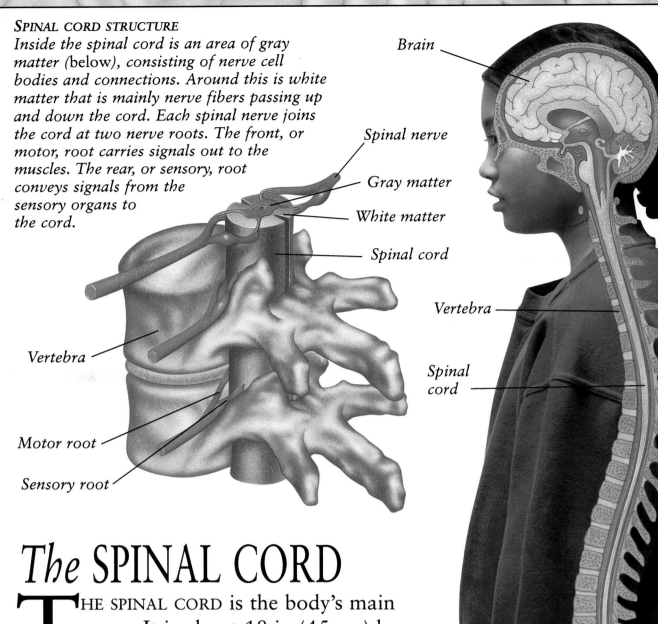

SPINAL CORD STRUCTURE
Inside the spinal cord is an area of gray matter (below), consisting of nerve cell bodies and connections. Around this is white matter that is mainly nerve fibers passing up and down the cord. Each spinal nerve joins the cord at two nerve roots. The front, or motor, root carries signals out to the muscles. The rear, or sensory, root conveys signals from the sensory organs to the cord.

Brain

Spinal nerve

Gray matter

White matter

Spinal cord

Vertebra

Vertebra

Spinal cord

Motor root

Sensory root

The SPINAL CORD

THE SPINAL CORD is the body's main nerve. It is about 18 in (45 cm) long and as thick as a finger. It extends from the tapered base of the brain inside a tunnel formed by a series of holes through the backbones, or vertebrae, that run down your spine (*above*).

The spinal cord acts as the link between your brain and the nerves that stretch throughout your body. Sprouting from either side of the cord are thirty one pairs of spinal nerves. These carry messages to and from the brain.

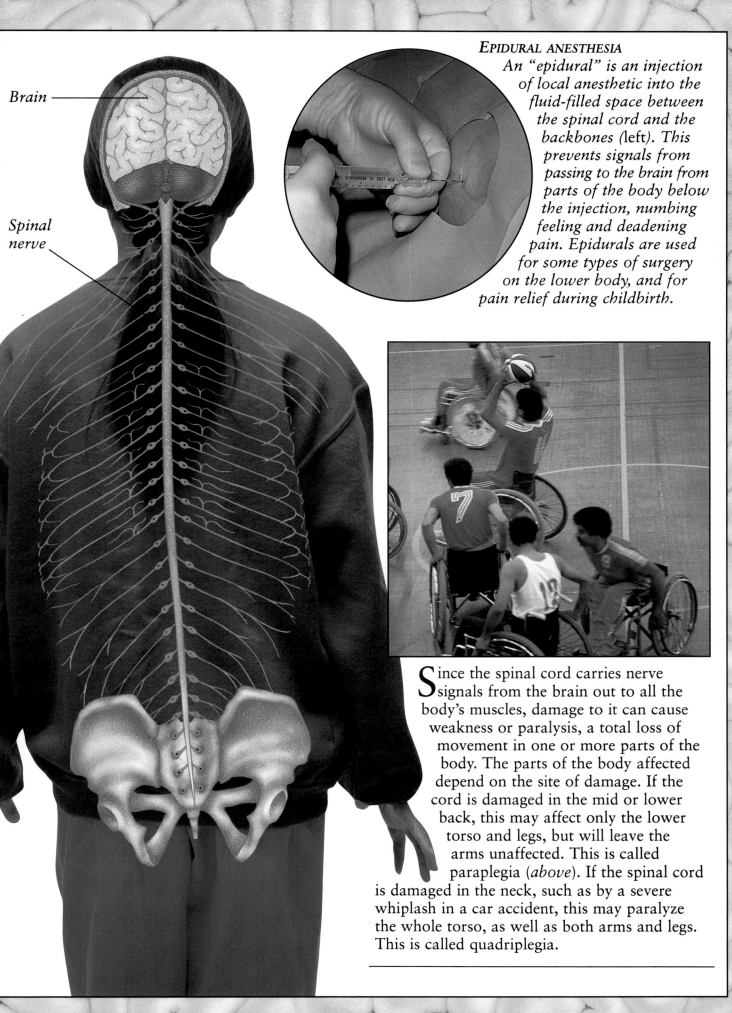

Brain

Spinal
nerve

EPIDURAL ANESTHESIA
An "epidural" is an injection of local anesthetic into the fluid-filled space between the spinal cord and the backbones (left). This prevents signals from passing to the brain from parts of the body below the injection, numbing feeling and deadening pain. Epidurals are used for some types of surgery on the lower body, and for pain relief during childbirth.

Since the spinal cord carries nerve signals from the brain out to all the body's muscles, damage to it can cause weakness or paralysis, a total loss of movement in one or more parts of the body. The parts of the body affected depend on the site of damage. If the cord is damaged in the mid or lower back, this may affect only the lower torso and legs, but will leave the arms unaffected. This is called paraplegia (*above*). If the spinal cord is damaged in the neck, such as by a severe whiplash in a car accident, this may paralyze the whole torso, as well as both arms and legs. This is called quadriplegia.

NERVES and NERVE CELLS

A NERVE is pale, tough, and stringlike, and resembles a living telephone wire. It carries millions of tiny electrical nerve signals every second. Your whole body has a massive number of these nerves and nerve cells — your brain alone contains more than 100 billion of them! They all have the same basic structure, but can vary in thickness and length tremendously. The sciatic nerve, in the upper thigh, is the body's thickest nerve, at 0.8 in (2 cm) wide. The thinnest nerves, in the toes and fingers, are narrower than the hairs on your head.

ASTROCYTES
These are star-shaped cells (above) found in the brain. They give shape, support, and nourishment to the delicate nerve cells and stop harmful substances from reaching them.

12

INSIDE A NERVE
A typical nerve has a tough outer covering, called an epineurium (below). Inside are the long wirelike fibers, or axons, of individual nerve cells, gathered into bundles called fascicles, wrapped in the perineurium (below and above). Each nerve has its own supply of small blood vessels.

Perineurium   *Fascicle*

Blood vessels

Epineurium

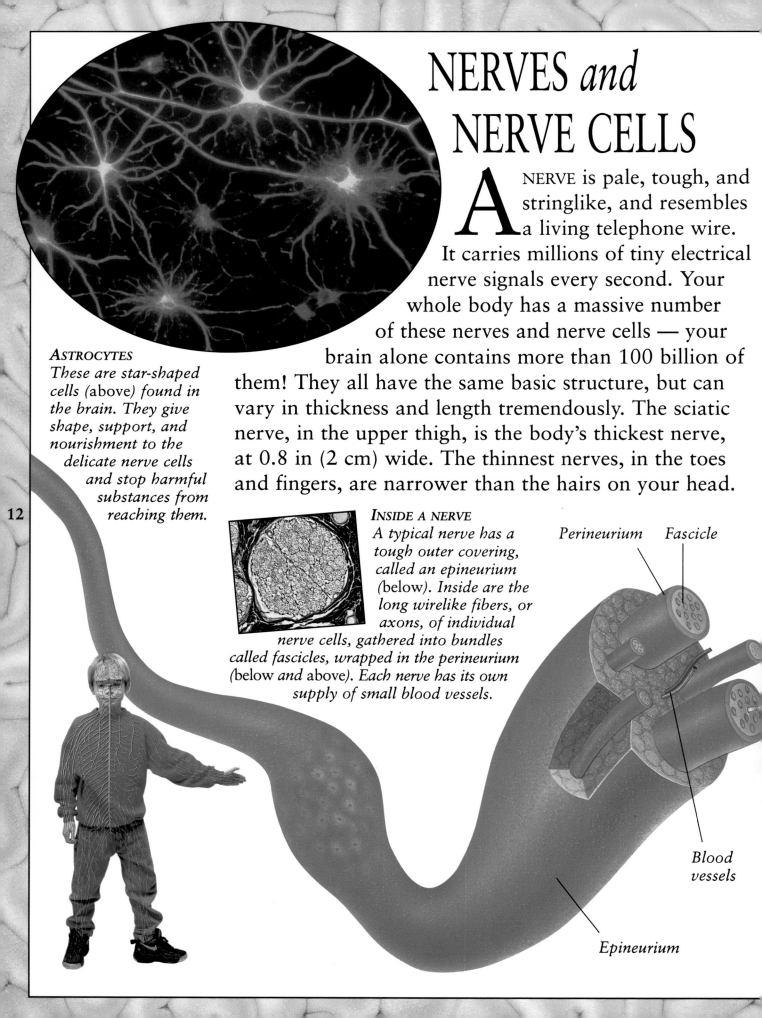

Cell body

Dendrite

Nucleus

THE NERVE CELL
The nerve cell, or neuron, has a main cell body with a nucleus (right). *Projecting from this are many short, spiderlike extensions, called dendrites. These receive nerve signals from other nerve cells. The signals pass around the cell body and down a very thin extension, the axon, to other nerve cells. In certain nerve cells, the axon is wrapped in a protective layer called the myelin sheath.*

Axon
(fiber)

Myelin
sheath

SHAPES
Nerve cells come in many shapes and sizes. These include multipolar nerve cells (right top) *with many short dendrites and one long axon, unipolar nerve cells* (right middle) *with the cell body on a side-branch of the main axon, and bipolar nerve cells* (right bottom), *where the long axon extends on either side of the cell body.*

In some accidents, nerves are severed. The result is numbness or paralysis of the cut part. These injuries cannot repair themselves. If the cut nerve ends can be carefully rejoined by micro-surgery, the patient may recover some sensation or movement. With careful treatment (*right*) the damaged part may recover completely.

HOW MESSAGES *are* SENT

A NERVE SIGNAL or message is a tiny pulse of electricity. It is only four-thousandths of one volt strong and lasts for just three-thousandths of a second. It travels not within the nerve cell, but along its outer "skin" or cell membrane. The nerve signal is created by the quick movement of electrically charged chemical particles, chiefly the minerals sodium and potassium, through the cell membrane.

When a nerve signal reaches the junction between one nerve cell and the next, called a synapse, a flood of chemicals is released. This passes the signal on to the next cell (*below*).

THE TRAVELING WAVE
In a large crowd, a "wave" (above) appears to travel along, but it is only people raising their arms. A nerve signal travels in the same way, as the result of movements of particles.

14

1 SYNAPSES
Where two nerves meet at a synapse they do not actually touch. Instead there is a tiny gap, called the synaptic cleft.

2 RECEPTORS
At a typical synapse (left), the bulgelike end of the sending neuron is extremely close to the cup-shaped portion of the receiving nerve cell. The surface of a receiving cell is covered with receptors.

3 NEUROTRANSMITTERS
A nerve signal arriving at the synapse triggers the release of chemicals, called neurotransmitters. These flow rapidly across the cleft and fit into the receptors. Once they have landed in these receptors, the next nerve cell continues the signal.

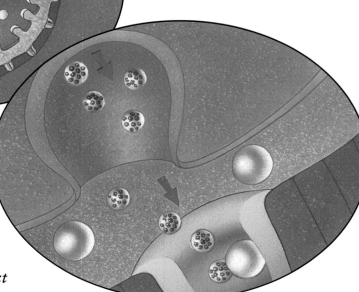

BRIDGING THE GAP

The synaptic cleft (left), where a nerve signal is passed from one nerve cell to another, is extremely narrow. It is usually about 1/500th the width of a human hair. A nerve signal can cross this gap in less than a thousandth of a second.

REACTION TIMES

Nerve signals travel quickly — about 330 feet per second (100 meters per second). However, this can still limit our reaction time to certain events.

For a sprinter to start a race, he or she must hear the sound of the starting gun and then send messages to the body's muscles to start running (left). Nerve signals will take at least one tenth of a second to travel from the ear to the brain and down to the legs. So a sprinter who sets off less than one tenth of a second after the gun has fired has made a false start. Race officials can check this by using sensitive equipment to measure the time between the firing of the starting gun and when the athlete leaves the blocks.

The sensation of pain is based on nerve signals that travel to the brain from the skin, other sense organs and sensors for pressure, damage, and other conditions inside the body. Pain-suppressing, or analgesic, drugs block the nerve pathways that conduct pain signals. They work by blocking the receptor sites on the synapses where messages are passed between nerve cells (*see left*). Doctors and dentists (*above*) can use analgesics as local anesthetics to deaden pain in a specific area.

The AUTOMATIC SYSTEM

IF YOU HAD TO REMEMBER to carry out every body process, such as telling your heart to beat, you would have little time left! The brain controls all of these processes automatically, like an autopilot in an aircraft. Most of this takes place in the lower brain — the brain stem, the midbrain, and the medulla. These send messages to body organs through a specialized network involving certain parts of the spinal cord and peripheral nerves. Together, these auto-functioning parts make up the Autonomic Nervous System, or ANS (*see* page 6). The ANS has two divisions, the sympathetic and parasympathetic (*see right*).

The pineal gland in the brain has nerve links to sense organs, especially the eyes. Scientists believe that it may automatically monitor signals from the eyes and then adjust levels of some chemicals in the body. One of these is melatonin, and its levels are affected by the amount of light that the eyes receive. The low light levels of winter may result in too much melatonin in the body. This can make people feel depressed and tired, a condition called SAD, or Seasonal Affective Disorder (*above*).

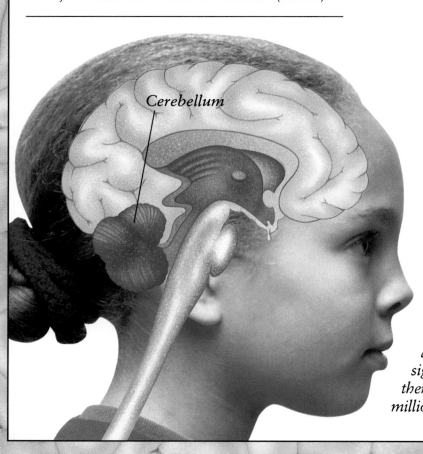

Cerebellum

DO IT WITHOUT THINKING
Skilled actions, such as playing a musical instrument (above) or sport, seem difficult at first. Yet after practice, we can do them almost without thinking. This is due to the cerebellum (left) that helps to make certain actions largely automatic. It receives general signals from the movement centers of the brain, then automatically fills in the details and sends out millions of signals to control hundreds of muscles.

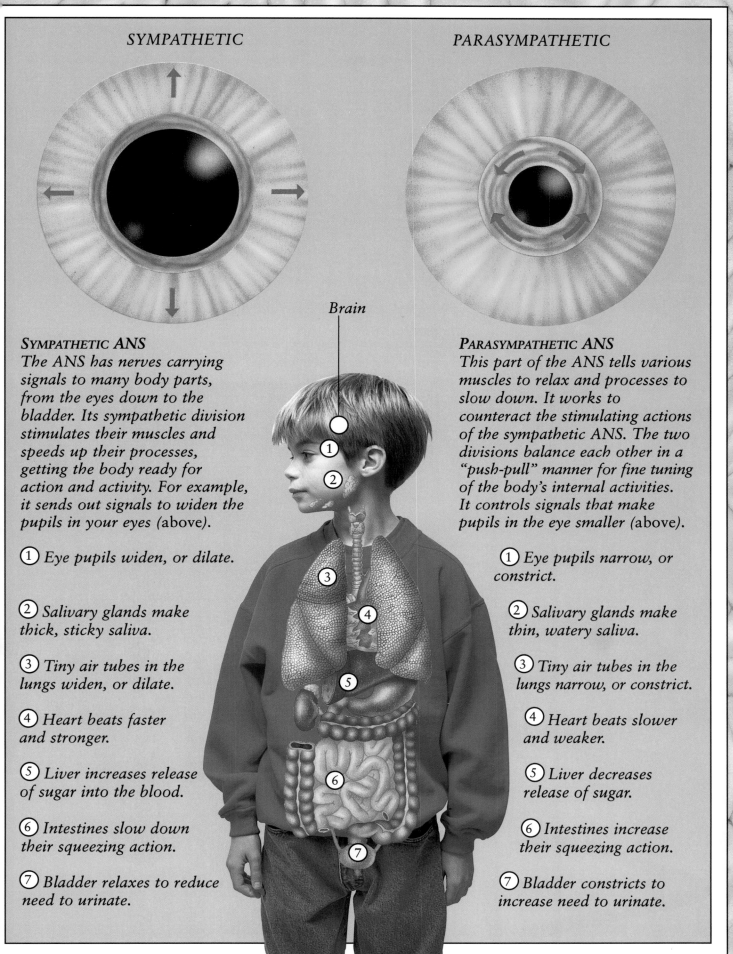

SYMPATHETIC

PARASYMPATHETIC

Brain

SYMPATHETIC ANS
The ANS has nerves carrying signals to many body parts, from the eyes down to the bladder. Its sympathetic division stimulates their muscles and speeds up their processes, getting the body ready for action and activity. For example, it sends out signals to widen the pupils in your eyes (above).

① Eye pupils widen, or dilate.

② Salivary glands make thick, sticky saliva.

③ Tiny air tubes in the lungs widen, or dilate.

④ Heart beats faster and stronger.

⑤ Liver increases release of sugar into the blood.

⑥ Intestines slow down their squeezing action.

⑦ Bladder relaxes to reduce need to urinate.

PARASYMPATHETIC ANS
This part of the ANS tells various muscles to relax and processes to slow down. It works to counteract the stimulating actions of the sympathetic ANS. The two divisions balance each other in a "push-pull" manner for fine tuning of the body's internal activities. It controls signals that make pupils in the eye smaller (above).

① Eye pupils narrow, or constrict.

② Salivary glands make thin, watery saliva.

③ Tiny air tubes in the lungs narrow, or constrict.

④ Heart beats slower and weaker.

⑤ Liver decreases release of sugar.

⑥ Intestines increase their squeezing action.

⑦ Bladder constricts to increase need to urinate.

17

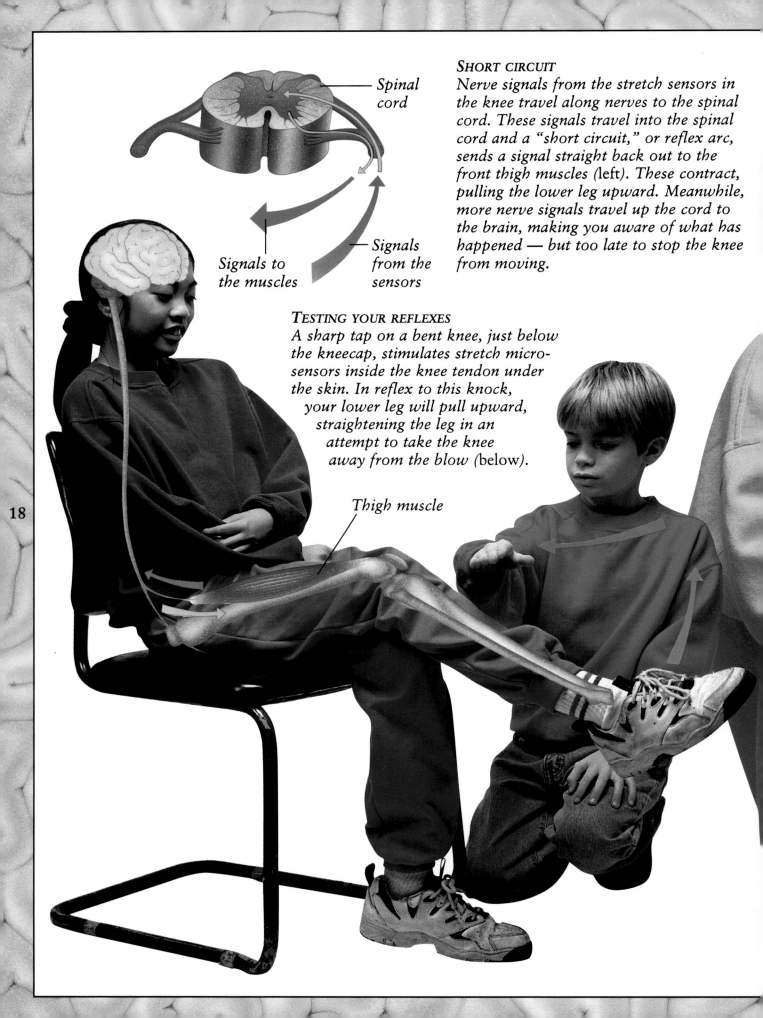

Spinal cord

SHORT CIRCUIT
Nerve signals from the stretch sensors in the knee travel along nerves to the spinal cord. These signals travel into the spinal cord and a "short circuit," or reflex arc, sends a signal straight back out to the front thigh muscles (left). These contract, pulling the lower leg upward. Meanwhile, more nerve signals travel up the cord to the brain, making you aware of what has happened — but too late to stop the knee from moving.

Signals to the muscles

Signals from the sensors

TESTING YOUR REFLEXES
A sharp tap on a bent knee, just below the kneecap, stimulates stretch micro-sensors inside the knee tendon under the skin. In reflex to this knock, your lower leg will pull upward, straightening the leg in an attempt to take the knee away from the blow (below).

Thigh muscle

18

BODY REFLEXES

A REFLEX is a body action or movement that occurs rapidly and automatically, in response to a certain stimulus detected by the senses. For example, if a piece of food moves to the back of your mouth, you swallow. If it gets stuck in your throat, you cough. If your hand touches something hot, you pull it away. If something gets stuck in your nose, you sneeze. These reflexes protect the body from harm. They occur without thinking or the need for conscious awareness.

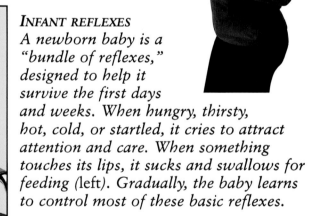

INFANT REFLEXES
*A newborn baby is a "bundle of reflexes," designed to help it survive the first days and weeks. When hungry, thirsty, hot, cold, or startled, it cries to attract attention and care. When something touches its lips, it sucks and swallows for feeding (*left*). Gradually, the baby learns to control most of these basic reflexes.*

Parts of the brain called the basal ganglia, deep inside the brain, are among the main processing centers for coordinated movements and actions. In Parkinson's disease (*right*), some chemicals are lacking in the basal ganglia. This causes rigid muscles and unusual movements, such as trembling of the arms and hands.

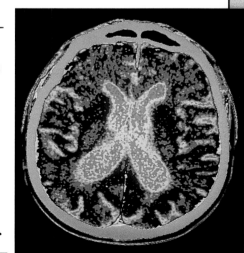

The THINKING BRAIN

AWARENESS AND ALERTNESS, thoughts and feelings, memories and emotions, and ideas and imagination are all based in the brain. Many occur in the wrinkled "surface" of the brain — the cerebral cortex. This grayish layer, about 0.2 in (0.5 cm) thick, consists of billions of nerve cell bodies and many trillions of their axons and dendrites, interconnected into a vast network. The cerebral cortex covers the white bulk of each cerebral hemisphere. It is where most of the functions of your everyday life are processed, from the touch of a feather to the movement of your arm. Each part of the cortex is responsible for sending out or receiving messages from a part of your body.

20

MOVEMENT CENTER
The movement center, or motor cortex, plans overall movements and sends out general instructions. The complex details of the movements, to make them accurate and precise, are added to and filled in by the cerebellum and other brain parts.

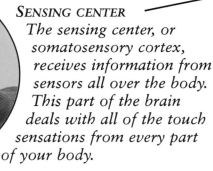

SENSING CENTER
The sensing center, or somatosensory cortex, receives information from sensors all over the body. This part of the brain deals with all of the touch sensations from every part of your body.

SIGHT CENTER
The sight center or visual cortex receives millions of messages each second along nerve pathways from the eyes. It decodes and analyzes them to create the three-dimensional color image of the world around us.

HEARING CENTER
The auditory cortex receives nerve signals from the ears and analyzes them to make sense of what we hear.

*D*yslexia affects the ability to learn to read and write. It takes various forms, such as seeing or writing letters of the alphabet back to front, swapping the order of letters, and even seeing words moving on the page. It can also involve a peroson's inability to "record" or memorize what is on the page. This, in turn, can lead to a very short attention span. Dyslexia has no link with overall intelligence. It may be overcome with early detection and special teaching methods (above).

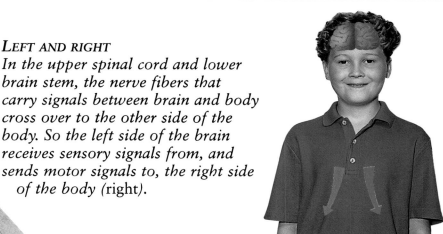

LEFT AND RIGHT
In the upper spinal cord and lower brain stem, the nerve fibers that carry signals between brain and body cross over to the other side of the body. So the left side of the brain receives sensory signals from, and sends motor signals to, the right side of the body (right).

21

SPEECH CENTER
A patch of cerebral cortex, called Wernicke's area, deals with the sense of written and spoken words. It lies on the side of the brain, toward the rear.

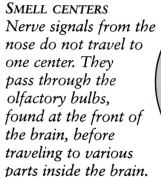

SMELL CENTERS
Nerve signals from the nose do not travel to one center. They pass through the olfactory bulbs, found at the front of the brain, before traveling to various parts inside the brain.

MEMORY *and* LEARNING

N O SINGLE SITE in the brain is a "memory center." Memories are probably formed, stored, reinforced, and recalled in various sites. These sites include the cerebral cortex, especially of the frontal and temporal lobes, and several structures within the brain, such as the hippocampus. It's believed that memories exist as routes or pathways along the nerve networks in these various areas. Each time you form a new memory, a new set of these connections is made. A single nerve cell can form links with more than 10,000 others, so the total number of possible pathways, and therefore the number of memories, is enormous.

REMEMBER TO LEARN
To learn something, we must memorize it first, in order to recall it later. We learn in an organized way at school (above), with lessons in a wide range of subjects. We also learn in daily life — how to identify things and behave in a certain way.

22

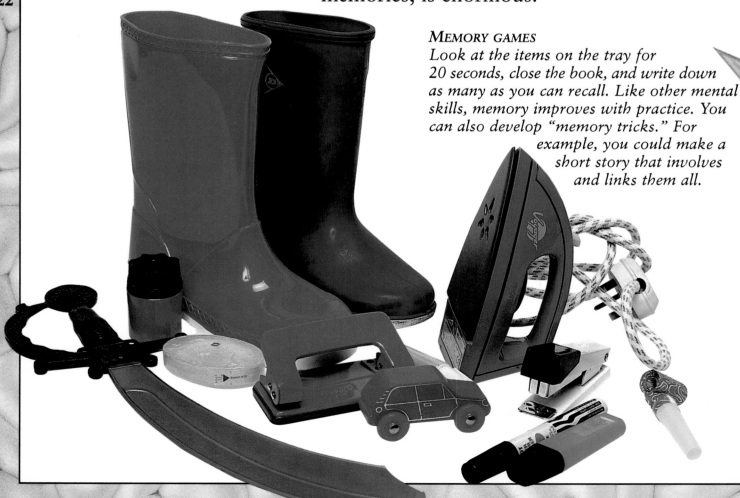

MEMORY GAMES
Look at the items on the tray for 20 seconds, close the book, and write down as many as you can recall. Like other mental skills, memory improves with practice. You can also develop "memory tricks." For example, you could make a short story that involves and links them all.

TYPES OF MEMORY

There are many ways of grouping or classifying different types of memory. A short-term memory lasts for a few seconds or minutes, only while it is needed. These can include looking up a telephone number, remembering something you have just read, or recalling the last meal that you ate (left). After they have been used, these memories are forgotten. Long-term memories last many years or even for the rest of your life. They usually contain significant information, such as your own address and your telephone number.

People who suffer damage to the hippocampus, found toward the center of the brain, are not able to make new long-term memories (*see below*). They can still recall events from long ago because the areas where these memories are stored are undamaged. But they cannot remember what they were doing a few hours or minutes previously.

THE HIPPOCAMPUS

Named because its shape resembles a seahorse, the hippocampus (left) is believed to help select significant short-term memories and convert them into long-term memories.

MOODS *and* STRESS

Stress has played a part in human lives for millions of years. Early humans had to face stressful situations that threatened their survival, although they were very different from the ones you face today. In response to these stressful times, nature has developed many mechanisms to help us deal with them.

Humans have also developed unique ways of communicating how we feel to each other. By using the intricate muscles in the face, people can show a wide range of moods and emotions, such as anger, joy, sadness, and grief (*below*). As part of our inborn behavior, these expressions are often "automatic," made without conscious effort or awareness.

24

FIGHT OR FLIGHT
This is one of the basic natural reactions to stress. When an animal, such as a dog (above), is confronted with something that it feels is threatening, it will react in one of two ways. It will either run away or stay and fight.

HOW STRESSFUL?

Scientists have graded stressful situations according to how they affect physical and mental health. At one end of the scale there are less stressful situations, such as starting school (right). Somewhere in the middle is a personal injury, such as breaking your leg. The most stressful situations usually involve personal loss, such as the death of a family member.

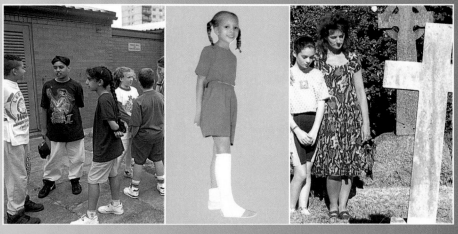

Cingulate gyrus

Fornix

Midbrain

Pons

Hippocampus

Amygdala

THE LIMBIC SYSTEM

The limbic system contains the fornix, the cingulate gyrus, the pons, the hippocampus, and the amygdala (left). It is also called the primitive brain, since it deals with very basic, animallike urges and emotions that aid survival, such as the fight and flight reaction (far left). These parts (above) lie deep inside the brain.

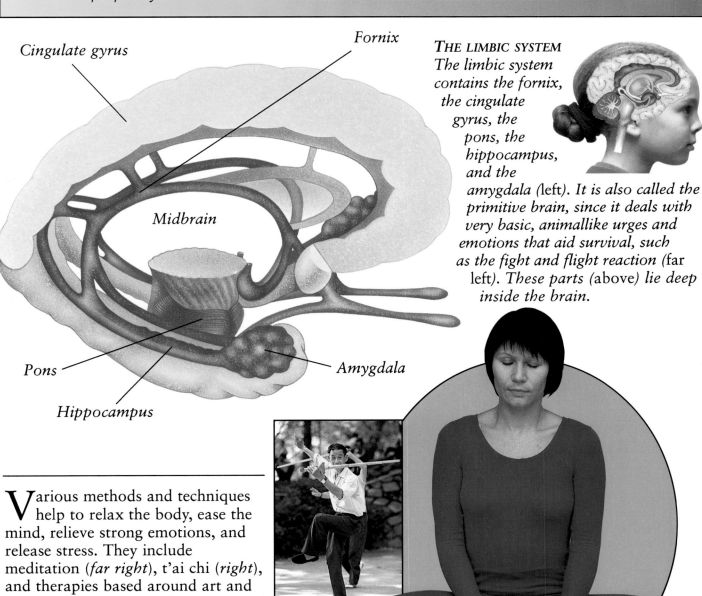

Various methods and techniques help to relax the body, ease the mind, relieve strong emotions, and release stress. They include meditation (far right), t'ai chi (right), and therapies based around art and music. The person may be encouraged to mentally focus on something simple, positive, and peaceful and so "empty the mind" of complex thoughts, problems, and emotions.

Awake

The need for sleep varies greatly, but on average it decreases with age. A new baby can sleep for up to 20 hours every day. A typical adult sleeps for eight hours each night, although some people need only three hours, while others require 12. Older people (left) may spread out their sleep by "cat-napping" during the day.

REM sleep

Deep sleep

SLEEPING CYCLES
Using EEG machines, scientists have discovered that you pass through "cycles" of various levels of consciousness during a night's sleep (right). These cycles last 80-120 minutes and their depth decreases until you wake up.

SLEEP *and* CONSCIOUSNESS

A sleeping person seems calm and relaxed. But the brain is still busy. Its electrical activity can be detected and displayed as wavy lines, or "brain waves," by an EEG machine (*see opposite*). As you sleep, your brain goes through levels of consciousness including deep sleep and Rapid Eye Movement (REM) sleep, which is usually when dreams occur. During REM sleep, your muscles twitch, your breathing becomes shallow, and your eyes move around quickly beneath your closed eyelids. These levels of consciousness are controlled by a part of the brain called the reticular formation. This lies deep inside the brain stem (*left*).

Reticular formation

Certain drugs and medications, such as caffeine in coffee (*right*), can have a stimulating effect on the user. They may increase alertness and arousal for a time, and delay the need for rest and sleep. But this is only a temporary effect, and can cause damage if continued.

— Awake

WAKING UP

A sleeping person's senses still send messages to the brain. Here, they are assessed for importance. A faroff vehicle or gust of wind are ignored. But significant events, such as the sound of a fire alarm (*above*), *make the reticular formation send signals to the upper parts of the brain that wake the sleeper.*

Awake

REM sleep

Deep sleep

THE EEG

The electro-encephalograph (EEG) machine detects the brain's electrical nerve activity. The tiny signals pass from the brain tissue, through the skull bone to the skin. They are picked up by metal sensors that are fixed to the head. These signals are displayed on a monitor screen or paper strip (*left*). The EEG traces show the various phases of sleep. The waves are close together during light sleep. In REM sleep they are shorter, more pointed and less regular (*above*).

BRAIN *and* NERVE DISORDERS

The brain and nerves may be affected by a variety of problems. Some are due to electrical faults and "wrong wiring" in the complicated networks of nerve cells and their connections. Others are based on chemical causes, such as the lack or excess of a certain neurotransmitter.

There are also emotional difficulties, that are concerned with the thought processes, rather than the brain's structure, chemistry, or electrical functioning.

Many brain and nerve problems, such as depression, epilepsy, and migraine, can be relieved by modern medical drugs, while psychotherapy and similar treatments can help treat many emotional difficulties that may occur.

28

MENINGITIS
An infection caused by meningitis bacteria (below) may lead to the swelling of membranes around the brain. This presses on the brain, causing headaches, nausea, and a stiff neck. If not treated in time, it can be fatal.

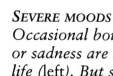

SEVERE MOODS
Occasional bouts of low mood or sadness are a natural part of life (left). But some types of prolonged depression occur for no obvious reason. They may be linked to problems in brain chemistry (see page 16). The depressed mood may alternate with exaggerated arousal and overactivity, known as mania. Doctors can treat some forms of depression by using mood-altering drugs, such as anti-depressants.

EPILEPSY

Epilepsy is like an "electrical storm" in the brain. Normal nerve cell signals (right top) become chaotic and random (right middle), which disrupts awareness and movement, often resulting in a fit or seizure. In grand mal epilepsy (right bottom), the disruption is so severe that the person may fall to the ground, lose consciousness, and make twitching movements for several minutes.

Brain blood vessels

MIGRAINE

Migraine headaches affect about one person in ten. Early in the attack, blood vessels in the brain and scalp (left) become narrowed. The severe headache that follows may also be preceded or accompanied by other symptoms, such as nausea, disturbed vision, or seeing blank patches. Some attacks may be triggered by stress, or even by certain foods or drinks, such as chocolate and alcohol.

A blow to the head may shake or jar the brain, and cause temporary loss of consciousness (*above*). This can be followed by dizziness, headaches, and memory loss.

A person who has suffered concussion — been "knocked out" — no matter how briefly, should consult a doctor within a few hours of the incident. There is a possible risk of further damage such as hemorrhage (bleeding) within or around the brain.

KNOW YOUR BODY!

NERVE CELLS *are some of the largest cells in the body. To get an idea of their scale, if the cell body were the size of a tennis ball, the axon (below) would be 0.6 miles (1 km) long. The net of dendrites that stretch out from the cell body would be as large as a tree (right). In real life, the longest nerve in the body is just 20in (50cm) long.*

IN AN UNBORN BABY, *1.25 million brain cells are produced every minute until it is born (left). By the time your body has matured your brain will contain 500 billion brain cells. After the age of 20 between 10,000 and 100,000 brain cells die each day.*

ALTHOUGH THE HUMAN BRAIN *weighs 3 lbs (1.4 kg), its effective weight is only 0.5 lbs (0.18 kg) because it is supported by fluid and membranes. Humans have one of the highest brain to body weight ratios, at 1:50. In comparison, a chimpanzee is 1:120 and a cow is 1:1,200 (below).*

THERE ARE *about 93,000 miles (150,000 km) of peripheral nerves that stretch to virtually every part of your body. The longest of these is the tibial nerve that is found in your leg (above). It stretches from your knee, down your lower leg, and into your foot.*

GLOSSARY

Anesthetic – A drug that numbs feeling in the body by blocking nerve signals to the brain.

Autonomic nervous system – The part of the nervous system that automatically controls the behavior of body parts, such as the heart, without you having to think about them. It has two parts: the sympathetic and the parasympathetic nervous systems.

Axon – A long, thin part of a nerve cell that carries nerve signals away from the cell body and on to the next nerve cell.

Brain – The tightly knit collection of nerves that sits inside your head.

Brain stem – The stalk of the brain that controls many of your body's automatic actions.

Central nervous system – The part of the nervous system that is made up of the brain and the spinal cord.

Cerebellum – This part of the nervous system sits underneath and to the rear of the rest of the brain. Its role is to refine and coordinate movement.

Cerebrum – The largest part of the brain. It has a wrinkled appearance and covers the surface. It is divided into two halves, called hemispheres.

Dendrite – The thin parts of a nerve cell that collect nerve signals and carry them to the cell body.

Ganglion – A clump or group of nerves that exists outside the central nervous system. There are 31 pairs of ganglia running down the sides of the spinal cord.

Lobe – General term for a region of the brain.

Memory – The ability to recall objects and events. It can be divided into long-term memory, involving distant or important objects and events, and short-term memory, involving recent objects and events that can be forgotten quickly.

Myelin sheath – A thick pad of insulation that surrounds and protects the axon of a nerve cell.

Parasympathetic nervous system – The part of the autonomic nervous system that tells muscles to relax and body activities to slow down.

Peripheral nervous system – The part of the nervous system that is made up of the nerves that shoot out from the brain and the spinal cord.

Rapid eye movement sleep – Also called REM sleep, this is a stage during sleep when your muscles start to twitch and your eyes move rapidly beneath your closed eyelids. It is also the time when you dream.

Spinal cord – The part of the central nervous system that stretches from the base of the brain, down through a tunnel in your vertebrae. It connects the brain with the nerves that run through the rest of the body.

Sympathetic nervous system – The part of the autonomic nervous system that stimulates the activity of body organs. For example, it makes the heart beat faster.

Synapse – The junction where two nerve cells meet.

Synaptic cleft – The tiny gap at the synapse that lies between two nerve cells.

Vertebra – The correct term for a backbone. Your whole spine is made up of some 26 vertebrae.

INDEX

Photo credits:
  Abbreviations: t-top, m-middle, b-bottom, r-right,
  l-left, c-center.

  All the pictures in this book were supplied by
  Roger Vlitos except the following pages:
  Front and back covers, 3tl, 9t & m, 11t, 12t & m,
  13, 15t, 19b, 27b, & 28m – Science Photo
  Library. 4, 5t & b – Bruce Coleman Collection.
  11m & 29br – Rex Features. 15m – Frank Spooner
  Pictures. 15b, 25bm & br – Spectrum Color Library.